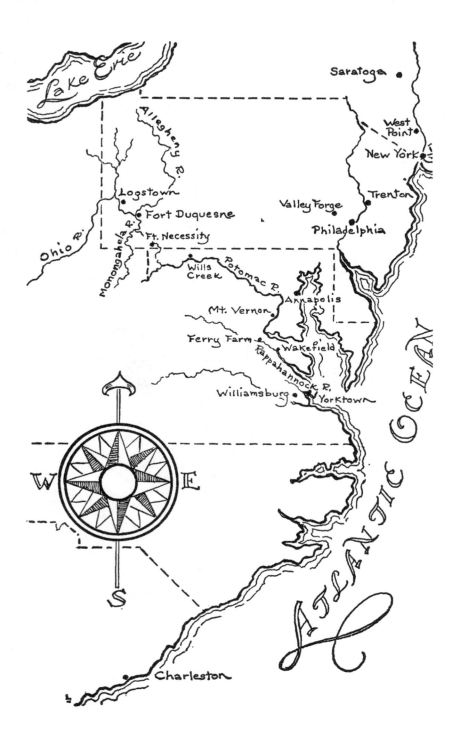

GEORGE WASHINGTON

FIRST PRESIDENT

ELSIE BALL

Illustrated by Manning de V. Lee

ABINGDON PRESS

New York • Nashville

To Johnny and Roy

"WAKEFIELD"

WASHINGTON'S BIRTHPLACE

CONTENTS

CHAPTER ONE

• THE MESSENGER •

On a day in early April in 1743, two boys walked briskly along the south bank of the Potomac River, in tidewater Virginia. A half dozen dogs, sniffing for foxes, ranged over the wide fields that stretched to the south and west.

"Cousin, how far does your land reach?" the younger boy asked.

"We don't know exactly where the boundary line should be, George," his cousin answered carelessly. "There's plenty of room for everyone. And besides all this, there are millions of acres in the new country on the other side of the Blue Ridge Mountains."

"I wish I could see that new country," George said. "Someday as many people may be living there as here along the Potomac."

The older boy shook his head. "I doubt it. Not many white people want to live among bears and rattlesnakes and wild Indians."

"I'd like to meet a real wild Indian," George replied.

"And you'd like to hunt bears and rattlesnakes, wouldn't you?" his cousin laughed. He glanced away across the fields and his expression changed. "Look, George, someone is coming!"

George's gray eyes narrowed as he caught sight of a man on horseback, riding in from the west.

"That's one of our horses!" he exclaimed. "I wonder what's happened! Mother said I could stay here until the spring school term began."

"Maybe your father's come home from

the ironworks," the older boy suggested.

"More likely he's heard of a ship that's sailing for England," George replied. "He's planning to send me there to school, so I can learn to be a gentleman."

"So soon?" asked the older boy.

"I'm eleven now," George said. "Almost as old as my half-brothers, Lawrence and Austin, were when they went to England."

The two boys whistled to the dogs and hurried toward the house.

The "mansion house" stood on a bluff high above the river. By the time the boys reached there, the traveler had arrived. His news was not what George had guessed. George's father, Captain Augustine Washington, was ill. The messenger had been sent to bring George home.

"What is the matter with my father?" George asked, as they rode westward toward Ferry Farm.

"He's sick, Master George. That's all I know," the Negro answered gravely.

"He must be very sick or he wouldn't have sent for me," George said.

"Don't worry, child," the man replied kindly. "Sick folks get notions. Master Gus got a notion he want to see you."

George thought this over for a minute. "My father's very strong, isn't he?" he said hopefully.

The sorrowful look on the man's face changed to a wide smile. "Master Gus sure is strong," he answered with a chuckle. "He's the strongest man I ever did see. I remember one day at the ironworks Master Gus told the men to load a big lump of iron onto a wagon. Two of them got hold of it and pulled and tugged. They couldn't even lift it off the ground. Master Gus shook his head, but he didn't say a word. He just pushed those two men out of the way. Then he lifted that piece of iron right into the wagon all by his self."

George's face brightened. "Father can do anything," he said proudly. "He goes to the ironworks, and he manages all his farms. He keeps accounts, and he buys and sells land. He can measure land, too, and tell where the boundary lines should be. I'd like to learn how to do that."

"You have to know how to cipher before you can survey land," his companion said.

"I like ciphering. I'll learn more when I go to school in England," George answered.

But George did not go to England. Soon after he reached Ferry Farm, his father died. George was left at the big frame house on the east bank of the Rappahannock River with his mother, his nine-year-old sister Betty, and his three younger brothers, Samuel, John Augustine, and Charles.

Like many men in Virginia at that time, Captain Augustine Washington had owned thousands of acres of land. Most of it he left to George's two grown-up half-brothers, Lawrence and Austin. He left George a large tract of land which was not very fertile. George was to receive this when he was twenty-one. Captain Washington also left Ferry Farm to George, but it was always used as the family home.

George realized that he would have to make his own way in the world. He thought a good deal about what he would do.

At last he went one day to a certain storehouse on the farm. This building held battered old tubs, extra kettles and pans, and other household supplies. Carefully, George opened the door. It was dusty and cobwebby inside. He took off his coat, folded it neatly, and laid it on a log. He put his hat on top of the coat. Then, with his sleeves rolled back, he went into the storehouse. Behind the pots and pans he found what he was

looking for. It was the tripod and the boxes that held his father's surveying instruments. George looked them over, piece by piece. Then he put them back in the boxes.

As he turned to leave, George found he was not alone. Standing beside the door was someone a bit smaller than himself. The little person was wearing a coat and hat like his, and had the same fair skin, gray eyes, and long nose.

George blinked. It was almost like seeing himself in a mirror. He looked again. Then he exclaimed, "Betty!"

His sister laughed gleefully. She took off George's hat and coat and shook down her long hair.

"What are you doing with Father's surveying instruments?" she asked.

"Mother says they are mine now," George answered. "When I know enough arithmetic, Mr. Byrne will show me how to use them.

"Betty, our men are making a treaty with the Indians. When that is done, there will be millions of acres of new land for people to buy. All that land will have to be measured off into farms and building lots. If I can do surveying, I shall be able to make a lot of money."

"What will you do with your money?" Betty asked.

"I will buy land, and raise the best crops and farm animals in Virginia," George answered.

"You will be a great planter someday," Betty said. She looked at him admiringly as they started back toward the house.

George could not go to a fine school in England now. But he still could go to Mr. Marye's school in Fredericksburg, across the Rappahannock River from Ferry Farm. George had always enjoyed arithmetic. Now he studied it very hard. He learned to draw neatly and to write clearly and rapidly.

George went beyond the usual school lessons in arithmetic. He was almost ready to study surveying, when his half-brother Lawrence suggested a different plan.

Lawrence had served on a British warship for a few years. He had liked the life of a naval officer. He thought it would be a more gentlemanly career for George than surveying.

George loved his kindhearted half-brother. He especially admired Lawrence's beautiful manners. In school George had copied a list of more than a hundred "Rules of Behavior" from an English book for boys. He always took pains to behave politely. He was willing to join the British navy if that would help him to become as fine a gentleman as Lawrence. But his mother said no.

Lawrence explained to her that in the British navy George could make a good living. He might even rise to a high position. Mrs. Washington still shook her head. She thought a sailor's life was too dangerous. Besides, she did not want her son to go so far away from her.

The argument went on and on. At last Mrs. Washington said to George, "I will write to your Uncle Joseph in London. He is older and wiser than Lawrence. We will do as he says."

It took a long time for letters to cross the ocean in the small, slow, sailing ships, and it was many months before an answer came back from Uncle Joseph Ball.

While they waited, George went ahead with his lessons in surveying. At last, when he was fifteen, the day came when he took the tripod and the instruments out of the storehouse. He found, to his delight, that he could actually measure land.

The first land he measured was a field that belonged to the schoolhouse. Then he measured other fields around Ferry Farm. Everywhere he went, he used his surveyor's instruments. Soon he began to get orders for work.

By the time Uncle Joseph's letter came, George had all the surveying jobs he could handle, and he was earning a good deal of money.

Uncle Joseph was definitely against George's joining the British navy. If George went to sea, his uncle wrote, he would be treated "like a dog."

That ended the matter. But Lawrence quickly went to work on a new plan — a plan which was to lead George into his first real adventure.

CHAPTER TWO

• ON THE FRONTIER •

Lawrence Washington and his wife Nancy lived at Mount Vernon, a plantation which overlooked the Potomac River. Nancy's family, the Fairfaxes, lived at a neighboring plantation called Belvoir.

A few weeks before George's sixteenth birthday he went to visit Lawrence and Nancy. George was now six feet tall and looked older than he was. He had broad shoulders, long arms, and large hands. He was strongly built, like his father.

"You came at just the right time," Lawrence told George. "Nancy's cousin, Lord Fairfax, is at Belvoir now. He owns millions of acres of the new land in the west. He will need a great many surveyors. We must let him know what you can do."

Then Lawrence asked George to measure his turnip field. "Let's go out and watch him," Lawrence said to Nancy.

Some of Nancy's family were visiting at Mount Vernon. They all watched as George set up his tripod and measured the turnip field. They all admired the neat diagram he made of it.

Not long after this, George rode to Belvoir. Lord Fairfax had already heard that George had measured Lawrence's turnip field. He offered George a job as helper with a surveying party that would soon start for the Shenandoah Valley. Nancy's brother was to be its leader. George was delighted to go, and his mother was willing.

Early in March, 1748, George started away on horseback with the others. He had learned to ride when he was a little boy, and was now an unusually good horseman.

The party headed toward the wilderness. The Indians had finally agreed to a treaty, so the frontier was less dangerous than it had been. But it still was wild. The surveyors usually slept in a tent or out of doors near a campfire. Sometimes a high wind blew the tent down. One night, when George was sleeping on a pile of straw, the straw caught fire. In spite of these mishaps, George found it better to sleep outdoors than in the rough cabins of the settlers.

The surveyors traveled northwest over trails that often were almost hidden by grass and weeds. Fallen trees blocked the way. Soon after the party reached the mountains, a heavy rain began to fall. Day after day it fell, until the rivers were flooded and the trails were slippery with mud. The men swam their horses across the Potomac, but found Maryland just as wet as Virginia.

At last they came to Cresap's trading post. This was located where Oldtown, Maryland, was later built. Here they rested for a day, while the rain still poured down. The next day the skies cleared, but the mud was too deep for the men to go on.

George spent the time cleaning up his clothes as well as he could, and writing in his diary. He was wondering what to do next, when suddenly a band of Indian braves appeared. They were decked out in war paint and feathers. They said they had been on the warpath against another tribe, but had taken only one scalp. They were quite unhappy about their poor luck.

The white men gave them some presents. This cheered up the Indians so much they decided to put on a dance. One of them took a gourd rattle, which swung from a bunch of horsehairs. Another borrowed a cooking pot

from Mr. Cresap, put water in it, and stretched a deerskin over the top to make a drum. Others gathered wood for a fire.

The Indians sat around the fire while their leader made a long speech in their Indian tongue. Then the dance began, with the drum and rattle for music.

George was delighted with the Indians. He tried to talk with them and learn all he could about their ways.

As soon as the ground was dry enough, the men went back across the river and started their surveying. The boundary lines of the grants of land were often marked by trees. George was especially helpful, because he knew the names of all the trees. He was pleased to find many hickory and walnut trees and groves of sugar maples. They would make this new country a pleasant place to live, he thought.

Sometimes the men cooked wild turkeys

for their campfire dinners. George enjoyed these dinners. One day he thought he would like to shoot a wild turkey. He fired at one, but the turkey did not drop dead. Instead, it ran away. George was astonished that such a big, awkward creature could move so quickly. He tried again, but he never had any luck shooting turkeys.

After this trip, George worked at his surveying and studied harder than ever. The next summer he helped to lay out the new city of Alexandria, Virginia. In the fall he went to the frontier country again for Lord Fairfax. He was now a commissioned county surveyor and in charge of all the men in the party. He was well paid, but he did not have such a good time as on his first trip. As quickly as he could, he finished the work and hurried back to Mount Vernon.

Lawrence had just returned from England, where he had gone to consult a doctor about a bad cough. While he was in London he had seen Uncle Joseph Ball. Uncle Joseph had sent Betty Washington a present — a silver tea set, with a chest of tea and a box of lump sugar.

"As soon as you get your chest, you can sit down and drink a dish of tea," Uncle Joseph wrote Betty.

Betty, like George, was growing up. A few months later, before she was seventeen years old, she was married to Fielding Lewis, a friend of George.

After Betty left home, George did not spend much time at Ferry Farm. Once in a while he visited his cousins, or his half-brother Austin. Several times he went back to the frontier to survey land for Lord Fairfax. He began to buy land for himself. Before long he owned several hundred acres in western Virginia.

Lawrence, too, was interested in the frontier. He was one of the head men in the Ohio Company which helped people settle on the land near the Ohio River. George often went on trips with Lawrence. Sometimes they were business trips and sometimes they were for Lawrence's health.

Lawrence's cough kept getting worse. The doctors told him that he must spend the winter where it was warmer. He decided to go to the island of Barbados, in the Caribbean. Nancy had to stay home with their baby daughter, Sarah. So George offered to go with Lawrence.

They sailed late in September, 1751. The ship was more than a month on the way. George watched the sailors at work and learned about the rigging and spars and sails. He kept a regular log of the ship's course, and noted every vessel he saw during the voyage.

Almost as soon as they landed on the

island, George caught smallpox. He was very ill for several weeks. When he was well enough to travel again, Lawrence said, "This climate is too hot and damp for either of us. You go back to Virginia. I will go to Bermuda."

So George returned to Virginia, and Lawrence went to Bermuda. But Lawrence did not get any better. Early in the summer he went back to Mount Vernon where he died a few weeks later. This was a dreadful blow to George, for he loved Lawrence dearly.

Lawrence had been adjutant of the militia for the colony of Virginia. This meant that he was responsible for training officers and drilling soldiers to be ready in case of war. George heard that Governor Dinwiddie was going to appoint three adjutants instead of one. He wrote the governor, asking for one of these positions.

"I should take the greatest pleasure in

punctually obeying your Honor's commands," he wrote, "and by a strict observance of my duty render myself worthy of your trust."

The governor and the council had already selected three older men. But they liked George Washington. They knew he was a young man who did his work well and who always kept his word.

"We may need someone like George Washington before long," they said.

They divided Virginia into four districts and made George adjutant of the fourth district. Just before his twenty-first birthday, George became Major Washington.

CHAPTER THREE

• CHIEF HALF KING •

George had often listened while Lawrence and Colonel Fairfax, Nancy's father, talked about war. He had watched Lawrence drill the militia. Now he spent all his spare time studying military tactics.

In the fall of 1753, bad news came from the frontier. The French, who held Canada, were coming south. They had built a fort on the southern shore of Lake Erie. They were making allies of Indian tribes which had been friendly to the English.

George hurried to Williamsburg, the capital of Virginia.

"If you wish," he said to Governor Dinwiddie, "I will go to the Ohio country and find out what the Frenchmen are trying to do."

The governor was glad to have George do this. He said that he had already sent two men to Logstown, later called Ambridge, Pennsylvania. There they had talked with Half King, an important Indian chief, who was a good friend of the English people. Half King believed that the French were planning to take possession of all the country near the Ohio River.

"First stop at John Frazier's trading post on the Monongahela River and talk with him," Governor Dinwiddie said to George. "Then go to Logstown and hold a council with Half King. Go on from there to the French fort. Give this letter to the French commander and tell him we expect a reply. Do not wait more than a week for it. While you are waiting, try to find out how many soldiers he has and what he plans to do."

The governor also gave George a letter to a famous frontiersman, Christopher Gist. Gist lived at Wills Creek, which later became Cumberland, Maryland. He had worked for Lawrence Washington in the Ohio Company. Gist agreed to go with George as head guide. George hired four other guides and a French interpreter.

On November 15, 1753, the seven men left Wills Creek. They followed a faint trail northwest over mountain ridges, through narrow valleys and laurel thickets, and across rushing streams. A week later, after being delayed by rain and snow, they came to Frazier's trading post. The trader had a message for them. Chief Half King had recently come to warn him that three tribes of Indians had gone on the warpath against the English settlers.

John Frazier told George that the French troops were in winter quarters near Lake

Erie. "You will have a long journey through the wilderness, and your horses are already tired," he said. "I will lend you a canoe."

The next day the guides paddled the baggage ten miles, to where the Monongahela joined the Allegheny River. From here two friendly chiefs guided George to Logstown. Half King was away hunting; they sent a runner for him.

George learned at Logstown that the French had built four forts on the Mississippi River.

Our people must act quickly, he thought. If they do not, the French will build forts over all this western country!

When Half King arrived, he promised to guide George and his party to the French fort. He was very angry with the Frenchmen. They had laughed at him when he warned them to leave the country. "This is our land and not yours!" Half King said he had told them, but they would not listen to him.

The next morning George made a speech before the chiefs and headmen of the village. He asked for warriors to go with his party to the French fort. But only two other chiefs and a hunter were willing to join Half King and go with George.

Half King said that first he must go to his hunting cabin and get a wampum belt which the Frenchmen had given him. He wanted to return it to show that he had broken his friendship with them.

It was four days before Half King was ready. On December 4, the party reached Venango, later Franklin, Pennsylvania. French soldiers occupied this town. While the chiefs held a council with the Delaware Indians, who lived nearby, George called on the French captain.

Captain Joincare invited George and his friends to dinner. The Frenchmen drank a good deal of wine, and talked very freely. They bragged that they were going to drive the English out of the country. They said that the Ohio and all its branches belonged to France, because the French explorer, La Salle, had discovered the river. George listened carefully to everything they said and wrote it all down in his diary.

Captain Joincare offered to send a French guide with George to the French fort. The next day a heavy rain delayed the start. Captain Joincare tried to make friends with the Indian chiefs and to keep them there, but at last the party set off. A French officer went with them as a guide.

The weather was now very bad. The men often had to chop down trees and lay them across the swollen streams in order to get to the other side. At last, on the evening of December 11, they came to the French fort.

George gave Governor Dinwiddie's letter

to the French commander of the fort.

The commander said that no Englishmen had any right to the Ohio River. But he was polite and offered to lend George a canoe so that he could get home more quickly.

George thought: There is something he does not want me to see!

When he left the commander, his guides met him. "The French have nearly two hundred pine canoes, and fifty birch canoes," they told George. "The soldiers say they are planning an expedition to the Ohio in the spring."

The commander gave George a letter for Governor Dinwiddie, and two canoes for the journey home. George had his men load one canoe with the baggage. He started three guides back to Venango by land with the tired horses.

But now Half King did not want to go. He said the Frenchmen had promised the

Indians guns if they would stay another day.

The next morning the Frenchmen tried to persuade the three chiefs to stay still longer. But they remembered their promise to guard George's party. Soon the two canoes were on their way down the river.

The three guides who had gone ahead with the horses were already in Venango when the men arrived in the canoes. George decided to start on at once. He asked Half King to go with him, but one of the other chiefs had been injured and Half King wanted to take him to Logstown in the canoe.

"Our hunter can go with you to keep you supplied with fresh meat," Half King offered.

"You are a good friend," George answered. "But you will need your hunter yourself."

The next day George and his party started south. It was bitterly cold. The horses could scarcely keep their footing on the ice and frozen snow. They traveled only five miles that day.

"Tomorrow we shall put our packs on the horses and we shall walk," George told the men.

Even with lighter loads, the horses moved slowly. A snowstorm made the way harder. Christmas Day came, and still the snow fell and still the half-frozen men and horses went on stumbling wearily along the trail.

At last George told the men to stop and build a shelter for themselves and the horses.

"They had better stay here until the storm ends," he said to Christopher Gist. "You and I will go on afoot."

George knew that Gist could take care of himself in the wilderness in any kind of weather. He had heard that one winter night, when Gist found a panther sleeping in a sheltered spot where he wanted to make camp, he drove the panther away, lit a fire, and slept peacefully in the panther's bed until morning!

Gist urged George to stay with the other men.

"I cannot wait," George answered. "In a few weeks the French will be moving south. I must get my report to Williamsburg."

He dressed in heavy woodsman's clothes, strapped a pack on his back, took his gun in in his hand, and started off with Gist.

That was a terrible day. Every bone and muscle in George's body ached with the cold. The ice in the streams was so thick it was hard to get even a sip of water. George and Gist marched on for eighteen miles. They slept a few hours in an empty Indian cabin, then they were up and off again.

They came to an Indian village. One of the Indians said he would show them a short cut over the mountains. He took George's pack, and they walked on for eight or ten miles. It was getting dark, and George wanted to stop and make camp.

The Indian promised to lead them to his cabin for the night. They followed him, but saw no sign of a cabin. Both George and Gist now believed that the Indian was leading them the wrong way on purpose.

Suddenly the Indian turned, lifted his gun, and fired at the two men. As he reloaded his rifle behind a tree, they seized him. They took the Indian's rifle and told him to walk ahead of them.

"We must get him away and then travel all night," Gist whispered to George.

Gist gave the Indian some bread and told him to go on and spend the night in his cabin and come back in the morning. He followed until he was sure the Indian had gone. Then he and George took up their packs and went on. They set a course by their compass and walked all night.

The next day they found Indian tracks in the snow. They decided it would be safer to walk separately, but when night came they met again. By this time they were ready to lie down and sleep, Indians or no Indians.

They expected the Allegheny River to be frozen hard enough for them to walk across. When they reached it, they found rushing water, choked with chunks of broken ice.

"We must build a raft," Gist said.

First they had to chop down a tree. As they had only one hatchet, George would chop for a while, then Gist, then George again. They worked all day. By sundown the raft was ready, with two long poles to guide it. They pushed it across the ice near the bank and launched it in the running stream.

The raft was scarcely in the water when the dashing current drove a pile of ice blocks directly in front of it. George tried to stop the raft by plunging his pole hard into the river.

The current drove the raft against the pole with such force that it jerked him off his feet and threw him into the icy water. Luckily George's arms were long, and his hands were big and strong. Somehow, as he fell, he managed to grab a log of the raft. He pulled himself up and scrambled back on the raft. But his pole was gone.

With only one pole, the two men could not

guide the raft either forward or back. They had all they could do to keep it from turning over in the tumbling, ice-filled water. At last the current carried them close to a small spot of land in the middle of the river, and they managed to wade to the island.

It was a wonder either George or Gist lived through that terrible night. The air grew colder every hour. The raft was gone. How they could get across the rest of the river they did not know. But the bitter cold, that had done them so much harm, at last did them a favor. In the morning the ice was solid enough to bear their weight. They crossed the river thankfully and walked the ten miles to Frazier's trading post.

John Frazier soon got a horse for George and he was on his way again. As he rode toward Williamsburg, he passed a pack train carrying building materials.

"The Ohio Company is going to build a fort

near Logstown," the driver told him. "The Company will send soldiers to guard the fort. Many new settlers are on their way to the new country."

On January 16, 1754, George Washington reached Williamsburg. He delivered the French commander's letter to Governor Dinwiddie. Then he stayed up most of the night to write a report of his journey.

The next day the report was read in the General Assembly of Virginia. The Assembly ordered George to recruit a company to guard the new fort on the Ohio, and promised to provide money for guns and supplies.

CHAPTER FOUR

• FORT NECESSITY •

Late in March, word came that eight hundred French troops were on their way to Logstown. The Governor of Virginia sent an order to George: "March what soldiers you have immediately to the Ohio."

George had about a hundred men. He needed horses and wagons to carry equipment and supplies. At last he got together twelve wagons and a few old horses.

Just as he and his men reached Wills Creek, a young officer, Edward Ward, and two Indians arrived. Ward had been stationed with forty men at the fort built by the Ohio Company. When he learned that a French army was heading toward the fort, he sent for help. No white men came, but Half King arrived with some Indians. They helped Ward and his men put up a stockade. Before it was finished, a thousand French soldiers appeared and ordered Ward to surrender. With so few men, he had no choice.

The Indians who had come to Wills Creek with Ward brought George this message from Half King: "If you do not come now, I think we shall never meet again. I speak with a heart full of grief."

George asked Ward and one Indian to take Half King's message to Williamsburg. He sent the other Indian back to Half King to tell him that help was on the way.

George and his company moved on slowly. The trails were not wide enough for wagons, so the men had to make roads as they went. They tried to travel down a river by boat, but falls and rapids stopped them. Rains delayed them. Worst of all, the food that was supposed to reach them did not come. Before long, all the flour was used, and the soldiers were close to starvation.

On the march, George kept meeting traders and Indians. Some of them had seen parties of Frenchmen nearby. George knew his few men could not take the fort on the Ohio away from the French soldiers. So he built a new fort at a place called Great Meadows, in what was later Fayette County, Pennsylvania. He named it Fort Necessity.

On May 24, Christopher Gist arrived at the fort. He told George that he had seen the footprints of French soldiers only five miles away. That night an Indian named Silverheels came to tell George that the Frenchmen were near Half King's camp, six miles away.

With Silverheels as guide, George led forty soldiers out into the rain. The night was so dark and the trail so slippery that even the

Indian guide often lost his way. It was almost morning when the men got to Half King's camp. About a dozen Indians were there, but few had guns. The Frenchmen were only half a mile away, in a camp hidden by rocks.

George's soldiers and the Indians crept silently through the woods and surrounded the French camp. The Frenchmen rushed out. Both sides fired at once. One of George's men was killed, and two were wounded. The French commander and nine of his men were killed. The others surrendered. George sent them under guard to Governor Dinwiddie.

Before long, word came that eight hundred French soldiers and four hundred Indians were on their way to attack Fort Necessity. For weeks George's men had not had enough sleep or enough to eat. Many of them were sick. Now, all who were able to work had to chop down trees and dig trenches to make the fort stronger.

Their Indian friends disappeared. Even Half King quietly slipped away. He was old and ill, and he saw that Fort Necessity could give little protection. It stood on low ground, with woods and hills around it. The Frenchmen could easily fire at it without risking their own lives.

On the third day of July, 1754, the French and their Indian allies opened fire on Fort Necessity. A heavy rain was falling. It seeped into cartridge boxes and ammunition. The trenches around the fort were running with water. George's soldiers were soaked to their skins.

Late in the day the rain suddenly increased, almost washing the men out of the trenches. Both sides stopped shooting. A voice called from the French side: "Will you send a messenger who can speak French? On our word of honor, he will be allowed to return unhurt."

After a long parley, George agreed to surrender the fort and to leave two men with the French as hostages. The next morning, which was the fourth of July, 1754, George and his soldiers marched out of Fort Necessity.

When this news reached England, a British general, with an army of regular British soldiers, was sent to drive the French out of the Ohio country. There did not seem to be any place in this new army for George. So he went to Mount Vernon, which Lawrence had left to him.

For a while George was busy buying furniture for the house and putting things in order on the land. But he kept thinking about the new expedition to the Ohio. He wrote a letter to welcome the British commander-in-chief, General Braddock.

General Braddock replied, offering George a place as his aide. George accepted. He left his young brother, John Augustine, in charge at Mount Vernon, and went to join the general. George was now twenty-three, and a colonel.

General Braddock had more men and more money for his army than George had ever had. But he had just as much trouble getting provisions. Traders sold him spoiled meat. They promised him flour and cattle and then did not deliver them. The farmers would not give up their horses and wagons. Benjamin Franklin finally got one hundred and fifty wagons in Pennsylvania for General Braddock. The soldiers had to cut down trees and build roads. Rain fell and turned the roads to mud.

The army had not gone far when George became very ill. For several days he rode in a baggage wagon, but the jolting of the springless wagon over the uneven, rocky road made him worse. At last General Braddock ordered him to stay behind until he was well. A week later, pale and weak, he was on his way again, and on July 8, he caught up with the army. They were now only about twelve miles from the fort, which the French had named Fort Duquesne.

Early the next morning the army set out on the final march. No enemy troops were anywhere in sight. General Braddock believed the victory was already won. His men were marching four abreast in a long column. They crossed the Monongahela River safely and were passing through an open forest.

Suddenly a wild Indian war whoop rang out. Guns sounded. Rifles cracked from behind trees and logs and rocks. Soldiers fell, killed or wounded without even seeing the enemy. Here and there American soldiers tried to fight the French and Indians in their own way, but there were too few Americans to drive back the enemy.

Hour after hour George dashed around the

battlefield, carrying orders from General Braddock to the officers and troops. He gave no thought to his own safety. Two horses were shot from under him. A bullet passed through his hat, and others made holes in his uniform, but he was not harmed.

General Braddock was not so fortunate. Five times a bullet struck down the horse on which he was riding. At last a shot reached him. As the sun went down, George and another officer got the general into a cart and across the river. Most of the soldiers who were left, including many of the wounded, were already across.

General Braddock ordered George to ride back to the British camp near Great Meadows for food and medical supplies. George was weak from his recent illness. He had already been in the saddle more than twelve hours. Yet all that dark night he rode over the rough trail through the wilderness. He managed to stay on his horse until he reached the camp, toward noon. There he delivered his message, and then slept for twenty hours.

General Braddock died on the way back east. George had his body buried in the road, where the tracks of horses, wagons, and marching soldiers would hide the grave from unfriendly Indians.

At Wills Creek, George's friends stared at him in amazement. They had heard that he had been killed in the battle!

As soon as he was rested, he went back to Mount Vernon. He thought he would never want to fight again. But he soon realized that somebody had to protect the frontier. There was no one now to hold back the unfriendly Indians. Every day reports came of attacks on the white settlers west of the Blue Ridge.

When Governor Dinwiddie asked George to take command of the Virginia regiment, he agreed. It was a hard, anxious task. With only seven hundred men he had to defend a frontier nearly four hundred miles long. More than once he narrowly escaped being captured or killed. He was constantly distressed by the terrible sights he saw.

After two long years of this difficult, dangerous work on the frontier, the doctor ordered Washington home for a rest.

When he was well again, he found a different situation. Early in 1758, the British government sent General John Forbes to lead the British forces in America in a new attack on Fort Duquesne. Besides the regular army, several of the colonies sent troops. Colonel George Washington was in charge of a regiment from Virginia.

General Forbes was a good soldier. He and his officers, including George, had learned a great deal from the mistakes that had been made before. As the army marched westward across the rough frontier country, the general tried to win over the unfriendly Indians. In this he had good help.

A missionary by the name of Frederick Post, who could speak the language of the Indians, had journeyed through the forest to persuade the red men to make peace. Although they did not like the British, many of the Indians were so impressed by Post's courage and honesty that they agreed not to fight.

Just as General Forbes and his army started on their last day's march, two Indian scouts came into camp. The French soldiers had left Fort Duquesne, they said, and the fort was on fire.

General Forbes ordered Colonel Washington to take some men and hurry ahead.

Washington found that the scouts' report was true. The Indian allies of the French had kept the promise they had made to Frederick Post. When the British troops drew near, they quietly disappeared, leaving the Frenchmen to hold the fort by themselves. The outnumbered French troops hastily set fire to the fort and hurried off down the river. Many of the Indians waited nearby to welcome General Forbes and his army.

The general ordered Colonel Washington to select men from his regiment to rebuild the fort and hold it during the winter. The French name, Fort Duquesne, was dropped and the fort was renamed Fort Pitt. Later, the city of Pittsburgh grew up where this frontier fort had stood.

CHAPTER FIVE

• MOUNT VERNON •

Washington left men to guard Fort Pitt, then started back to Virginia. It was a difficult journey. All the way he fought December winds and deep mud.

At Williamsburg Washington made sure that the soldiers of the Virginia regiment would promptly receive their pay and the supplies they needed. Then he resigned his military commission.

Washington's heart was light as he mounted his horse again and headed for a big plantation twenty-five miles northwest of Williamsburg. He was due there for an important occasion — his own wedding. The bride, Martha Dandridge Custis, was a widow with two little children — Jackie, aged four, and two-year-old Patsy. Washington was free now to settle down as a farmer. He planned to take Martha and the children to Mount Vernon. There they would have a pleasant home together.

The wedding was on January 6, 1759. Washington had a number of things to do before he could take his new family to Mount Vernon. Martha and the children had inherited a good deal of property. Washington felt he should study their business affairs so that he could look after them.

He had been elected a member of the House of Burgesses of the General Assembly of Virginia, which made the laws for the colony. It was about to meet, and Washington had to be present. So in February, he took his bride and the children to Williamsburg with him. As Martha owned a house there, the famiy had a real home in the Virginia capital.

Washington was greeted warmly by the other members of the House of Burgesses. They passed a resolution praising and thanking him for his "faithful services" and his "brave and steady behavior" during the war. Washington was pleased but greatly embarrassed. He rose to answer but could not find words to express his feelings.

"Sit down, Mr. Washington," the Speaker of the House said. "Your modesty is equal to your valor, and that surpasses the power of any language that I possess."

At last, in early April, Washington and his family set out for Mount Vernon. They took a number of Martha's servants and a heavy load of trunks and boxes. When they were almost there, Washington suddenly realized that his house was not ready for them. It had been closed up for months and was sure to be cold and damp and dusty. Most of the furniture had been stored away. There was no comfortable place to sleep or to eat.

Washington hastily wrote a letter to his farm manager, John Alton. He sent it on ahead by a messenger on horseback.

"You must have the house very well cleaned," the letter said. A long list of instructions followed. Bedsteads must be set up and beds made, tables and chairs cleaned and put in place, the staircase polished, and fires laid in the fireplaces. He also wrote John Alton to get eggs and chickens from the neighbors, and have them prepared "in the best manner you can."

Probably John Alton did not know much about house cleaning. But he quickly put all the servants to work. When Washington brought his bride to her new home, the place did not look too badly neglected.

But Martha Washington had her own

ideas. After a few days she sent an order to
Williamsburg for new furniture, carpets,
curtains, and draperies.

Washington found a great deal to do on
the plantation. His brother, John Augustine,
had done his best to take care of it, but he had
to leave long before Washington's return.

Crops had failed; hogs had been stolen; fences had fallen down.

Washington repaired the buildings and fences and bought new animals for the farm. He liked fine farm animals and raised many. He worked hard to make his land pay.

At first, like most Virginia planters, Washington made tobacco his principal crop. But within a few years he was raising a great deal of wheat. There were two watermills on the plantation, and he kept them busy much of the time grinding his own grain. He even shipped flour to England and the West Indies. It is said that his flour was so good that a barrel with the name "G. Washington" stamped on it was passed in foreign ports without the usual inspection.

Washington experimented with crop rotation years before most farmers thought of doing this. He had many fruit trees on his land, and cultivated apple and cherry and apricot orchards. He liked to work with fruit trees and especially enjoyed pruning and grafting them.

He did not neglect the river that flowed by his home, either. In the seasons when fish were plentiful, he had a fishing boat on the Potomac. The servants salted down all the herring and shad which could be used on the plantation. Washington sold the rest.

Neighbors and tenants came to Washington's blacksmith shop at Mount Vernon to have their horses shod and their plows and wagons repaired. Often they paid their bills with butter or eggs. One man who needed a good deal of blacksmith work done traded a brown cow for it. Another man paid for his work by doing tailoring and knitting socks. In return for a large supply of pork, a neighbor painted a boat for Washington.

Colonel Washington put down all these items in his ledgers. He tried to treat everyone fairly and wanted to be treated fairly himself.

All over Virginia Washington became known as a wise and just man. People turned confidently to him when they had difficult problems. A tenant farmer, in debt and in danger of having his possessions sold, hurried to Mount Vernon to borrow the money from Colonel Washington. A hired workman, wanting to bring his family from the old country, asked Washington to advance the money.

Washington's well-to-do neighbors often asked his advice. He helped to settle their estates, and he lent them money.

He never neglected his relatives. When his mother became too old to manage Ferry Farm, Washington built her a house in Fredericksburg, near Betty's home. He took over the management of the farm himself, but sent all the income to his mother.

And no matter how busy he might be, Washington did not forget the men who had served in his regiment. When they came to Mount Vernon, they were always given a welcome and a good meal. If they were in need, Washington would give them money.

He worked out a plan by which he hoped to benefit them, and himself as well. In 1754, Governor Dinwiddie had promised land in the unsettled west to the soldiers who fought for the Ohio River fort. When this part of the country was opened up for settlement, Washington insisted that the governor's promise must be kept. After much delay, the Virginia government agreed.

Washington made a trip to the Ohio country to help select and survey the tracts of land to be distributed. Every private soldier was given the right to four hundred acres. The officers, including Washington, received larger grants.

Washington now owned several thousand acres of land. Part of this land was rented to tenant farmers. Part was cultivated by overseers, under Washington's own supervision. Much of it was new land that was being cleared, a little at a time, when men could be spared to do the work.

As most farm tasks were done by hand, Washington needed many workers. Some were white men, hired for wages or working on commission. Most were Negro slaves, as on the other large Virginia plantations.

Washington provided good food and clothing for his slaves and cared for them when they were ill. At one time smallpox broke out among the slaves on one of his farms. Because Washington had had smallpox, he could not get it again. So he himself went to look after the Negroes who were sick.

Washington had always been used to the system of slavery, but he felt that it was wrong. As the years went by, his dislike for it increased. "There is not a man living who wishes more sincerely than I do to see a plan adopted for the abolition of slavery," he wrote to a friend.

He was much interested in the idea that machinery might someday be used for the heavy, backbreaking farm tasks. In a farm publication he found a description of an "engine," something like a stump puller, which would lessen the toil of clearing the land. Washington never was able to get hold of this contrivance, but he did try his skill in making a new kind of plow. Alas for his hopes! The plow was too heavy for a team of horses to pull through damp ground.

Washington did not try again to be an inventor. More important matters were crowding upon his time.

CHAPTER SIX

· DIFFICULT DAYS ·

The General Assembly of Virginia, which made the laws for the colony, was made up of the Council and the House of Burgesses. The Council members were appointed by the British government. The members of the House of Burgesses were elected by the people of Virginia. The Governor of Virginia, who was appointed by the British king, had the power to call the Assembly together or to dismiss it. He could also veto any laws it passed.

Washington was a member of the House of Burgesses. He went to Williamsburg every year for its meeting. He was there in 1765, when news came of a Stamp Act, passed by the British Parliament. The British government was badly in need of money, especially for its army, and it had decided to raise part of this money by taxing the American colonies. The Stamp Act said that the colonists must put a special stamp on every record of a sale or any other business transaction. Some of these stamps, which the colonists had to buy from England, were quite expensive.

In the House of Burgesses, where Washington was sitting, a plainly dressed young lawyer named Patrick Henry stood up. He read a set of resolutions that he wanted the House to send to King George III. These resolutions pointed out that the royal charter of the colony granted the Virginians all the rights of other Englishmen. Among these was the right to be taxed only by themselves or their representatives. The Stamp Act was unconstitutional, Patrick Henry said, because the colonies had no representatives in the British Parliament.

A number of the members of the House of Burgesses did not agree with Patrick Henry. Some believed that Parliament did have a right to tax the colonies. Others were afraid to oppose the British government. "Wait and see what happens," they said.

Patrick Henry rose again. He said that the Stamp Act was the act of a tyrant. He named rulers who had been put to death for their harsh acts.

"Caesar had his Brutus," he shouted, "Charles the First his Cromwell, and George the Third . . . "

The Speaker of the House stopped him, exclaiming, "Treason!"

Patrick Henry calmly finished his sentence: "and George the Third may profit by their example." Then he added, "If this be treason, make the most of it!"

The Speaker again rebuked Patrick Henry, but his resolutions were adopted.

Washington saw and heard all this. He went back to Mount Vernon deeply disturbed. In a letter he spoke of the Stamp Act as "unconstitutional" and "ill judged." He knew that if England enforced it, the Americans would refuse to carry on any business with the English. Then overseas trade would stop, and the Americans would have to depend on themselves for everything. They would have to weave their own cloth and make their own tools.

Some cloth was already being woven at Mount Vernon, and some tools were being hammered out in the blacksmith shop. Washington made plans to have more such work done on his plantation.

Soon Washington learned that in all the colonies men were getting ready to resist the Stamp Act. In October, delegates from nine colonies met in New York to protest against it. There were angry gatherings in Williamsburg, too. Planters refused to send their grain and tobacco to England, because the ships could not leave without having stamped papers. People wore their old clothes and sharpened up their old tools and got along without goods from overseas.

The next spring the colonists had welcome news from England. Parliament had repealed the Stamp Act. British merchants had asked Parliament to do this, because they were afraid of losing their entire trade in America. Now once more ships could sail back and forth across the Atlantic, carrying goods from one country to the other.

Parliament still insisted, however, that it had the right to make laws for the Americans and to tax them as it chose. Now it put taxes on paints, glass, paper, and tea.

When the Virginia Assembly met, the

House of Burgesses prepared a protest against the new taxation. The governor did not like this, so he dismissed the Assembly. The House of Burgesses did not give up. Its members met in another building to discuss what to do.

Washington had given considerable thought to this matter of taxation. Now he presented a plan. In the other colonies, he said, men were forming associations and pledging themselves not to buy certain English goods until the new taxes were removed. He had brought an agreement of this sort with him, which he suggested the members sign. Nearly all of them did. Among those who signed Washington's agreement was the youngest member of the House of Burgesses, Thomas Jefferson.

The British Parliament soon realized that it had made another mistake in dealing with its American colonies. It hastily sent word that all the taxes would be removed, except the tax on tea.

This satisfied some Americans, but most of them, like Washington, still refused to buy the taxed tea. Then the British law-makers thought up another scheme. They arranged to sell tea in America so cheaply that even with the tax it would cost less than it did in England.

The people of Massachusetts quickly saw that Parliament was trying to prove its right to collect taxes from the colonists. When three ships loaded with the low-priced tea entered Boston Harbor, a number of men dressed themselves up like Indians and went on board the ships at night. With whoops and yells they dumped the tea into the water.

The British government took care of this by closing the port of Boston to all ships until the city paid for the tea.

Washington heard this news while he was

in Williamsburg, attending the Assembly. Like all the other men in the House of Burgesses, he was greatly concerned.

The members of the House agreed to spend the first day of June, 1774, the day on which Boston Harbor was to be closed, in "fasting, humiliation, and prayer." This was to be done so that they might have "one heart and one mind" to defend their rights, and that the king and the Parliament might be "inspired from above with wisdom, moderation, and justice."

The Governor of Virginia was displeased. Again he dismissed the Assembly. Again the House of Burgesses met in another place. This time it voted to ask the other colonies to help organize a "general congress." This congress would meet each year to consider "the united interests of America."

On the first of June, as agreed, Washington went to church and fasted all day. He had sent a letter from Williamsburg to the minister of his home church, asking him to hold special services on that day. Washington realized that tremendously important events were taking place.

During the summer Washington spent most of his time helping to organize the new "general congress" of the American colonies. He was one of the seven delegates sent from Virginia to the congress in Philadelphia in September. Representatives from twelve colonies attended and organized the Continental Congress.

Washington listened earnestly as men from the different colonies told about their troubles with the British. The delegates voted to send help to the poor people of Boston, who had been thrown out of work by the closing of the port. They also voted that after December 1, 1774, the colonies should stop all trade with England. Before they left, they agreed to meet again in Philadelphia the next May.

Washington saw clearly that a hard struggle was coming. As soon as he got back to Virginia, he began to drill a company of militia. His brother, John Augustine, did the same. This was a dangerous thing to do. Men who rebelled against the British might be hanged as traitors.

But Washington was not afraid. He wrote to John Augustine: "It is my full intention to devote my life and fortune in the cause we are engaged in, if need be."

Some of Washington's friends tried to persuade him not to oppose the British. They argued: "The English have a powerful navy. They can control all the country along the Atlantic Coast. They have the best equipped army in the world. We have no navy. We have no trained army. We have little equipment, and no way of manufacturing any. We have almost no money. The British will surely win."

Washington answered that if the Americans were driven out of their homes in the east, they could find new homes on the other side of the mountains. He was sure they could hold that western land for themselves.

In April, 1775, bad news came from Massachusetts. British soldiers had fired on American volunteers in Lexington and Concord. Eight men had been killed and more were wounded. Reports said that American volunteers had chased the British back to Boston and were keeping them shut up there. But everyone knew the American volunteers could not hold out very long unless they had help from the other colonies.

CHAPTER SEVEN

• COMMANDER-IN-CHIEF •

In May, 1775, the Continental Congress met again in Philadelphia. Washington went dressed in the red-and-blue military uniform he had worn during the French and Indian War. He wanted everyone to know that he was willing to help the cause of American freedom in any way possible.

The Congress voted to raise an army to resist the British. Then John Adams of Massachusetts said he wished to nominate a general for the army.

He said he had only one person in mind — a gentleman from Virginia.

Washington looked startled.

This gentleman, Adams went on to say, was one "whose skill and experience as an officer, whose independent fortune, great talents, and excellent character would command the approbation of all America, and unite the cordial exertions of all the Colonies better than any other person in the Union."

Washington rose, confused and embarrassed, and hurried out of the room.

The next day, June 15, 1775, he did not go to the meeting. In the afternoon some of the other delegates met him. They shook hands with him and called him General.

"You were elected unanimously as commander-in-chief of all the continental forces, raised, or to be raised for the defense of American liberty," they told him. "No one else was even considered."

Washington had been quite willing to lead a Virginia regiment. But to be head of the entire army! To oppose, with untrained men, the military and naval strength of Great Britain! That, he thought, was too heavy a task. Yet he did not say no.

He thanked his friends for the honor they had shown him. "I do not think myself equal to the command," he said. "However, as the Congress desires, I will enter upon the momentous duty, and exert every power I possess in their service for the support of the glorious Cause."

Washington refused the five hundred dollars a month Congress voted to pay him.

"I do not wish to make any profit," he said. "I will keep an exact account of my expenses. Those, I doubt not, they will discharge; and that is all I desire."

In the midst of selecting officers and making plans for the new army, Washington took time to send letters and gifts to his wife. Two years before this, her daughter Patsy had died. Her son Jackie was married. Washington was afraid Martha would be very lonely while he was away.

"I do not know whether it may be in my power to write you again till I get to the camp at Boston," he told her. "I go fully trusting in that Providence which has been more bountiful to me than I deserve and in full confidence of a happy meeting with you sometime in the Fall."

He wrote to his farm manager, too, sending him instructions and naming a sum to be used for needy persons who came to Mount Vernon for help. "Let no one go away hungry," he wrote.

Washington was almost ready to start on the long ride to Boston when he heard bad news from that city. There had been another and more serious clash between the British and the Americans. Many soldiers on both sides had been killed.

Washington knew that there was no time

to lose. With a few officers and a mounted escort, he set out on his first journey as commander-in-chief of the American army.

A messenger from Boston met Washington and his companions as they were leaving Philadelphia. The messenger had more details of the battle. He told Washington that the American soldiers guarding Boston had heard that the British were going to attack them. On June 16, twelve hundred American soldiers stationed themselves on a hill just outside the city. The next day British soldiers attacked them and drove them off the hill. This looked like a victory for the British, but it was a costly one. They lost a thousand men in this Battle of Bunker Hill.

This news made Washington very anxious to get to Boston as quickly as possible. On the way, however, he had to stop in New York to meet the people there and to plan for the defense of that city.

Thousands of people gathered at the New York ferry to greet him. Among them were several groups of volunteer soldiers. They welcomed him with joyful shouts and proudly led him and his aides through the streets of the city. Washington looked every inch the general in his fine blue uniform with a purple sash and a plumed hat. He had heard that there were many Tories — people who were loyal to England — in New York. Now he discovered that there were also many true American patriots.

From New York Washington hurried on to Boston. The British still held the hill which they had taken. But they had found out how well the Americans could fight, and they had not tried to go any farther.

This was fortunate, for Washington soon realized that the Americans were not ready for a war. The soldiers were wonderful marksmen but they were not used to working together. They needed training. They also needed food and clothing. Most of all, they needed ammunition.

Washington could not risk a battle because the men were unprepared. He did not dare to say much about this, for fear the British would hear what a sorry state the

American soldiers were in and destroy the entire army. He sent secret messages to the president of the Congress in Philadelphia and to the governors of some of the colonies. Then, while they were trying to get ammunition for the army, Washington organized and drilled the soldiers.

By the next March, after eight months of training, the army was at last ready to fight. Washington acted quickly and boldly. One night he sent troops to occupy a hill, Dorchester Heights, which overlooked the city and harbor of Boston. The men could not dig trenches in the frozen ground. Instead, they hid behind movable frames, covered with bundles of hay and brush.

In the morning the British saw these covered frames. They thought they were great earthworks.

"Washington must have a big army. It would take fifteen thousand men to build such defenses overnight!" the British soldiers said. They felt that they were trapped. After a few days of confusion, they boarded their ships and sailed out of the harbor.

The people of Boston were free at last! The Massachusetts Assembly thanked the "good and great" General Washington for what he had done. He was praised by the selectmen of Boston and by Harvard University. A young Negro girl, Phyllis Wheatley, sent him a poem she had written about him. Washington answered her in a very kind letter which he signed, "With great respect, your humble servant, George Washington."

Washington felt sure that now the British army would try to take New York. So he hurried there with his soldiers. They quickly built forts at several points near the city.

The war was spreading. The British tried to capture Charleston, South Carolina, but were beaten off. Washington sent an army to guard the northern part of the country. One of his most trusted officers, Colonel Benedict Arnold, led an expedition into Canada.

The Americans were now manufacturing some ammunition and buying some from other countries. But they still did not have enough for the entire army.

Many Americans were still loyal to England. Others simply did not care which way the war went, so long as their own affairs seemed to prosper. This made it hard for the Congress to raise money to pay the soldiers and to provide them with proper food and clothing. Washington was kept busy long hours every day, trying to solve these problems.

Early in the summer of 1776, something happened in Philadelphia that startled everyone in America. On July 4, the Continental Congress approved a document called the Declaration of Independence. The news reached Washington's headquarters in New York on July 9. Washington ordered the men of the different brigades to line up on their parade grounds at six o'clock that evening. In front of each brigade stood an officer, holding a copy of the document. In a loud voice the officer read the Declaration of Independence. The soldiers cheered and shouted. They were no longer subjects of the English king; they were citizens of a free country!

Crowds gathered in the streets of New York to celebrate the good news. A statue of George III on horseback stood on a high pedestal in a park. With ropes and bars a group of American patriots pulled it down. Other patriots hauled it away into Connecticut to be melted down into bullets for the American army.

A day or two later a fleet of British ships sailed into New York harbor. On them were the British soldiers that had left Boston and the soldiers that had been in the south. Other British ships soon arrived, bringing more troops. Some of these were hired soldiers from Germany, called Hessians.

Now came several months of defeat and discouragement for the Americans. Washington's army was driven out of Long Island, then out of Manhattan, across New Jersey, and finally over the Delaware River into Pennsylvania. Many American soldiers were killed or captured. Many others deserted.

By the end of 1776, Washington had only a few soldiers left. These men were poorly clothed and hungry. They had little ammunition and less hope. Most of them were simply waiting for their term of enlistment to end. In December, 1776, it seemed as if the entire American army would soon fall to pieces. The effort for American independence seemed to be coming to a miserable end.

On the other side of the Delaware River

from Washington's army was the village of Trenton. It was being held by Hessians. They were waiting there for the river to freeze hard enough so they could march across and wipe out Washington's little army.

Washington made a bold plan. Somehow he got hold of some large, flat-bottomed boats. On Christmas Day he divided his army into three parts. One part he sent nine miles up the river. One part he stationed directly opposite Trenton. The third part he placed farther down the river. He ordered each force to cross the river that night. Once over, they would join in an early morning attack on the Hessians in Trenton.

The northern force was led by Washington himself. For hours the men worked in the bitter cold, loading cannons and horses on the boats. Then the soldiers stepped into the boats, and sailors from Marblehead took up the oars. The skillful sailors guided the boats across the wide river, through the darkness and snow and the drifting blocks of ice. At four o'clock in the morning the last boatload of American soldiers landed on the New Jersey side. They were shivering with cold and weariness. Ahead of them lay the nine-mile march to Trenton. The two other forces had been unable to make any headway against the storm and the floating ice. Only this one part of the army had succeeded in carrying out Washington's plan.

Snow was falling, sleet and rain covered the roads with ice. The men's clothes were thin and their shoes were worn and broken. Here and there a streak of blood showed where a soldier's foot had been cut by the jagged ice. But the men marched bravely along.

Many of the Hessians had been celebrating Christmas by drinking a great deal of liquor. They were scarcely awake when the Americans reached the camp at Trenton and opened fire on them. Heavy headed, confused by the attack and blinded by the storm, the Hessians were in no condition to fight.

The battle was soon over. By ten o'clock that morning every Hessian in Trenton had surrendered. That day Washington took more than nine hundred prisoners, without the loss of a single American life.

When the British general, Lord Cornwallis, heard of this victory of Washington, he hurried toward Trenton. He brought with him a good-sized army.

The American soldiers retreated into the New Jersey woods. They kept the British soldiers away by firing at them from behind trees, Indian style. When the British made camp, Washington put some of his men to work tending campfires and digging trenches nearby. He wanted to make the British think that his whole army was staying there that night. He left the sentinels and camp guards there. Then, in the darkness, he marched the rest of his troops past the British camp and on to Princeton. They captured Princeton and drove out three British regiments.

These successes saved the American army. Most of the soldiers cheerfully enlisted again, and many new men entered the service.

During the next year Washington himself won no victories. But one of his officers, General Gates, defeated the British General Burgoyne at Saratoga, New York. This was one of the greatest victories of the Revolution.

That winter Washington went into camp at Valley Forge. It was the hardest winter of the war. The officers in charge of supplies did not know how to handle their job. They let supplies pile up in storehouses while the soldiers suffered. The food given to the troops was scanty and poor. Their clothing was thin and ragged. Half of the soldiers had no blankets and nearly half were barefooted.

Some of the men who were able to work in the cold chopped down trees and built log huts. The others did not have enough clothing to venture out of their miserable tents. They huddled "on a cold, bleak hill," Washington wrote, and slept "under frost or snow without clothes or blankets."

Many of the officers were as ragged as the men. For three long, cold months the men suffered bitterly. It was a wonder they stayed in the army. But they had come to believe, like Washington, that the American cause was right and that, in the end, they must surely win.

CHAPTER EIGHT

• VICTORY AT LAST •

Early in the spring of 1778, good news came across the Atlantic. The French government, which was at war with England, was sending ships and men to help the Americans. Lafayette, a young French nobleman, had come to America earlier to help the new country in its struggle for freedom.

When the British heard this news, they became alarmed. They realized that the French fleet could easily sail into the harbor of Philadelphia and shut off the British troops there from their supplies. So the British hastily left Philadelphia and went to New York.

On their way, Washington attacked them.

At the point of victory one of his own officers, an Englishman named Charles Lee, disobeyed Washington's orders and allowed the British army to escape.

Philadelphia was now back in the hands of the Americans. Washington built a line of forts west of New York to protect the interior of the country. Benedict Arnold, a trusted officer in the American army, turned traitor and tried to surrender the West Point fort to the British. His treachery was discovered in time to save the fort, but Arnold managed to get away safely to a British ship.

The British next sent an army, commanded by Lord Cornwallis, to conquer the southern states. He had some success at first, but the southerners at last drove him north to Yorktown, Virginia.

Washington had sent Lafayette south with a small army to oppose and annoy the British forces. Now Washington, with his army reinforced by five thousand French soldiers, hurried south to meet Lafayette and stop Cornwallis at Yorktown.

The American army besieged Cornwallis and his men by land. At the same time the French fleet sailed into Chesapeake Bay and cut off British escape by sea. Their food and ammunition gave out. There was no way of getting any fresh supplies. After two months of suffering and hardship, in October, 1781, Cornwallis surrendered to Washington.

This victory practically ended the fighting. But the British continued to hold New York, and for two more years it was necessary for Washington to keep his army ready for any possible British action.

The soldiers grew very restless during this time. A number of young officers thought up a plan to make Washington king of the new country. Washington was hurt and angry at this idea. He wrote to the young men that their plan filled him "with horror." He ordered them to "banish these thoughts" and never speak of them again.

At last, in September, 1783, peace was made between England and the United States. Each of the thirteen states was recognized as "free, sovereign, and independent." A few weeks later the last of the British troops left the American shores.

Washington and his soldiers marched into New York. There was a week of rejoicing, with many speeches praising Washington and his men. On December 4, 1783, Washington's officers met him at Fraunces Tavern to bid him good-by.

The street outside the tavern was crowded with men, women, and children, waiting to get a look at the general. Washington was greatly touched. He could not smile or speak. He could only wave his hand in farewell.

After stopping in Philadelphia and Baltimore, he went to Annapolis, Maryland, where the Continental Congress was in session. On December 23, 1783, he appeared before it.

The crowded room was hushed as Washington read his resignation as commander-in-chief. He thanked the people who had served with him and helped him.

"I consider it an indispensable duty," he read, "to close this last solemn act of my official life by commending the interests of our dearest country to the protection of Almighty God, and those who have the superintendence of them to his holy keeping."

His voice broke. He waited a moment, then went on, ending his speech: "I here offer my commission, and take my leave of all the employments of public life."

He handed his speech and his commission to the presiding officer of the Congress. After bows and handshakes, he mounted his horse and set off for Mount Vernon.

CHAPTER NINE

· WRITING THE CONSTITUTION ·

General Washington was now simply George Washington, Virginia planter. Once more he was coming back from war to the place he loved best. This time he reached Mount Vernon the day before Christmas.

Many things had changed since he rode away to Philadelphia, eight and a half years before. His stepson, Jack Custis, had taken cold while helping him during the siege of Yorktown and had died a few weeks later.

But even with Jack and Patsy gone, the home was not empty. Jack's two little children, Parke and Nelly Custis, were waiting with their grandmother to give Washington a joyful welcome. His favorite servants crowded around, eager and excited. It was the happiest Christmas Washington had known in many years.

With great satisfaction Washington took up farming again. This was the occupation he most enjoyed. He found a great deal to do. During the war his fields and orchards had been neglected. The fences and farm buildings were run down. The lawns and gardens needed attention.

Washington began at once to make the necessary repairs. He fertilized his fields and tried out new and different crops. He experimented with crop rotation. He straightened the fences, and put up new buildings. He pruned and grafted his fruit trees. He enlarged his house and added paved walks and colonnades. He landscaped the grounds. He carefully designed two curving driveways, and bordered them with trees.

Although Washington had resigned as commander-in-chief, he was not yet through with the army. Many of the soldiers had received little or no pay for the time they spent in the service. Washington worked hard to get their back pay for them. But by the time they were paid, the money had gone down in value and was worth very little. So Washington and some of his friends persuaded the Continental Congress to allow the soldiers to trade their poor money for good land in the Ohio country.

In September, 1784, Washington went on horseback with a pack train to look over the new land in the northwest. He himself owned several thousand acres there. He wished to see his own land. He also wanted to set aside tracts to be divided into farms for the soldiers who wished to settle there. He slept outdoors and helped with the surveying, just as he had done when he was a young man.

The country west of the Blue Ridge Mountains was now filling up with settlers. These pioneers were very independent. They did not recognize the authority of any government.

Washington understood why they felt so free. In the peace treaty, the British government had named each state separately, as if the thirteen states were thirteen different nations. This left the Continental Congress with little authority to enforce the law in the new lands.

Washington realized that a foreign army could easily take all this pioneer country if the settlers had no recognized government. He saw, too, that the thirteen states would not be free and independent very long unless they were united. Already they were quarreling among themselves.

As soon as Washington got back to Mount Vernon, he sent letters to the governors and

influential men in the different states. He urged them to form a central government. "Something must be done," he wrote, "or the fabric must fall, for it certainly is tottering."

In May, 1787, delegates from twelve states met in Philadelphia to plan a union. This meeting was called the Constitutional Convention. Washington was unanimously chosen to be the presiding officer.

For four months the men studied and debated how the new country could best be governed. There were many difficult problems.

The Convention agreed on a law-making Congress with two parts — the Senate and the House of Representatives. In the Senate each state, whether large or small, would have two members. In the House of Representatives the number of members from each state would be in proportion to the population of the state.

The Convention considered the office of president. How should he be elected? Should he hold office for life? Should there be a number of presidents, each one with different duties?

All through these discussions, Washington said little. But the delegates constantly watched his face and relied on his wisdom to guide them in making the right decisions.

At last, after four months of very hard work, the Constitution of the United States was written and offered to the American people. The people accepted it eagerly. They were glad to have some settled form of government, so that they could begin to make plans for the future.

Before the end of June, 1788, nine states had agreed to the Constitution, and it became the law of the land. Instead of thirteen little separate nations there was now one great nation, the United States of America.

CHAPTER TEN

• FIRST PRESIDENT •

Mount Vernon had become a place of unusual beauty. It was the sort of home that Washington had been hoping and planning for ever since he was a boy. He had spent many years away from it, serving his country. He hoped that now at last he could settle down quietly on his beloved plantation and live the kind of life he most enjoyed.

But Washington's country still needed him. Someone had to organize the government of the new republic and guide it until it was really established. No other man, the American people thought, could do this as well as George Washington. No other man was so beloved in America or so greatly respected in foreign countries. And so, early in 1789, George Washington was unanimously elected as the first President of the United States.

Once again Washington bade a regretful farewell to Mount Vernon. Before leaving Virginia, he rode to Fredericksburg to see his mother. It was his last visit to her. She died a few months later.

Washington journeyed north, to New York, the national capital. All along the way people greeted him joyfully. They put up triumphal arches for him to ride through, and the children strewed flowers before him.

When he came to the New Jersey shore, across from New York, a special barge was waiting. Thirteen masters of vessels, one for each state in the Union, rowed him across the Hudson River. Cannons boomed out a welcome for the first president as he stepped ashore. George Clinton, Governor of New

York, met him and rode with him through streets bright with flags and lined with cheering people.

On April 30, 1789, a great crowd gathered near Federal Hall, in New York, to see their first president inaugurated. Standing on a balcony, Washington took the oath of office. The watching men, women, and children listened in silence. When the ceremony ended, they broke into shouts of joy.

New York was not the only place that celebrated the inauguration. All up and down the thirteen states there was rejoicing. The American people felt safe with Washington at the head of their new nation.

Washington felt deeply the honor and the responsibility of being president. In his inaugural address he said he was "overwhelmed" by "the magnitude and the difficulty of the trust to which the voice of my country called me." He believed that the

United States had a special destiny. He felt that "the preservation of the sacred fire of liberty, and the destiny of the republican model of government" were "finally staked on the experiment entrusted to the hands of the American people."

Washington wanted the public to realize that he was equally interested in every section of the country. In 1789 and 1790, he traveled through the northern states. In 1791, he visited the South.

The President of the United States, Washington felt, should conduct himself with as much dignity as the head of any other country. So, everywhere he went, he took great pains to dress well and to use formal manners. He wore a black velvet suit with gold buckles and carried a hat with an ostrich plume. He rode in a gilded coach drawn by four cream-colored horses.

In 1790, the nation's capital was moved to

Philadelphia. The new government was slowly taking shape. Many highly gifted men held
important positions in it. One of these was
Thomas Jefferson, author of the Declaration
of Independence. Another was Alexander
Hamilton. He established wise and honest
financial policies that made the United States

respected in other lands, and encouraged commerce and manufacture.

In 1792, Washington was elected, unanimously as before, to a second term of four years as president. During this time, France and England went to war with each other. Washington's great concern was to keep America out of war. He wanted the new country to have a chance to develop and grow strong. So he issued a proclamation of neutrality.

This proclamation of neutrality and a treaty which was made about a year later with the British were very unpopular with the Americans. Many of them thought they should stand by the country that had helped them win their independence. Many thought they should not become friends with England so soon. Bitter speeches about Washington were made in Congress and harsh articles were printed in newspapers.

But when the time came to select a president again, the people once more turned to Washington. They asked him to accept a third four-year term. This time he refused.

On September 19, 1796, Washington read his farewell address before the House of Representatives. In it he warned the lawmakers against quarrels among the different sections of the country. Their best interests, he said, lay in "carefully guarding and preserving the Union." They must cherish the principles of religion and morality. They should abide by the Constitution. They should "steer clear of permanent alliances" with other nations, since such alliances might lead to war.

In March, 1797, Washington gave up his duties as president and started happily back to Mount Vernon.

CHAPTER ELEVEN

· HOME AT LAST ·

Washington had been very much hurt by the cruel things that had been said about him. But on his journey back to Virginia he found that the American people still loved and admired him. All along the way they gathered to greet him with welcoming words and gifts. Flags waved, men cheered, old people blessed him, and children brought spring blossoms to brighten his way.

As always happened after he had been away, he found a great deal to do at Mount Vernon. Every morning he got up early and rode around his farm on horseback to see what was going on. In the afternoons he worked in his study. There he kept his accounts, read and wrote letters, and kept up with the news.

Washington was astonished to find how famous he had become. People came from all over the world to see him. Sometimes they waited for hours just to catch a glimpse of him.

Many of the visitors at Mount Vernon were old friends, or important persons. They were likely to be impressed both by Washington's stately manners and by his kindness. He was always strictly on time. If guests came late for dinner, Washington would say, "Gentlemen, we are punctual here. My cook never asks whether the company has arrived, but whether the hour has."

He showed much concern for the comfort of his guests. One overnight visitor complained of having a cold. At bedtime he heard a knock on his door. Opening it, he was

amazed to see Washington himself bringing
a steaming hot cup of tea.

All this was pleasant, but it did not give
Washington the quiet and rest that he
wanted. He wrote to a friend that he never
had a meal alone with his family.

For a while it looked as if Washington

might have to leave Mount Vernon again. A quarrel with France made war seem possible. President Adams called on Washington to serve once more as commander-in-chief. Washington had a handsome new uniform made, and went to work to organize an army. He was greatly relieved when the danger of war blew over.

Once again he could give his whole time to his plantation and his friends. He liked to have young people around him. His nieces and nephews and their friends and the children of his friends came to visit at Mount Vernon and sometimes stayed for years.

One of the young guests was the son of his old comrade, Lafayette. Because Lafayette had insisted on law and order during the French Revolution, he was captured and put in prison. His friends sent his sixteen-year-old son, who had been named for Washington, to America. Washington gave the boy a home at Mount Vernon until his father was freed, and then paid his way back to France.

Of all his young friends, Washington's favorite was Nelly Custis, Jack Custis' daughter. She had lived with him and Martha Washington, her grandmother, ever since she was a tiny child. She was with Washington a great deal. She went riding with him. She went to church with him. She played on her harpsichord and sang to him.

Washington was much pleased when Nelly became engaged to his sister Betty's son. A grand wedding was planned for her. Washington promised to wear a military uniform at the wedding. But he did not wear his fine new uniform. Instead, he came dressed in the old uniform which he had worn during the uncertain, difficult days of the war.

Nelly understood why he had done this. The new clothes, fine as they were, meant little to him. But the old uniform brought back memories of many great days. They reminded him of the day when he had entered New York at the head of his victorious army, and of the day when he had stood in the State House in Annapolis and resigned his commission. Nelly realized that he considered her wedding day another great day in his life. She threw her arms around his neck and thanked him for showing her such great honor.

Washington once said that he expected to live until 1800. This did not quite come true.

On December 12, 1799, he rode out as usual to look over his plantation. During the morning the weather became very cold. A rainstorm came up. The rain turned to hail, and the hail to snow. Washington was out in the storm for several hours.

The next day he had a cold. He paid little attention to it. "Let it go as it came," he said.

On the following day, he was much worse. Doctors were called, but could do little for him. Washington knew that the end had come. "I am not afraid to go," he said.

When the news of his death reached Congress, the lawmakers arranged a great memorial service and procession. All citizens of the United States were asked to wear mourning bands on their left sleeves for thirty days. In every state the people paid tribute to his memory. In the words of Henry Lee, he was "first in war, first in peace, and first in the hearts of his countrymen."

Even the nations he had opposed in war joined in the mourning. Both the British fleet and the French army officially recognized the passing of a great man.

Washington left instructions in his will that his slaves were to be freed. Those who were too old or too feeble to work could have a home at Mount Vernon as long as they lived. Or, if they wished to spend their last days in some other place, they were to receive an allowance for living expenses. The children were to be protected and given enough schooling and training to fit them to earn a living.

Mount Vernon was made into a national shrine. Each year thousands of people visit it.

But we do not need to go to Mount Vernon to find a memorial to Washington. The national capital of the United States is named for him. Across the continent, on the Pacific Coast, is a great state called Washington. Thirty-two counties and almost as many small cities and towns bear the honored name. And there is scarcely a town of any size in all the land that does not have its Washington Street or Washington Avenue or Washington School.

George Washington was fortunate in seeing most of the great projects for which he worked accomplished during his lifetime. Thousands of settlers found safe, pleasant homes in the land beyond the Blue Ridge Mountains. The thirteen colonies scattered along the Atlantic coast became a unified, powerful country. Best of all, it was a free country, ruled by the people themselves.

Many wise and courageous men and women helped to bring these things to pass. But Washington's part was the noblest of all. He was the master builder of the new nation. As commander-in-chief during the Revolution, as a framer of the Constitution, and as first President of the United States, he was truly the Father of his Country.

CPSIA information can be obtained
at www.ICGtesting.com
Printed in the USA
BVHW060035010921
615695BV00015B/1713